A Certain
WOMAN

SHARON COVINGTON

A Certain
WOMAN

ARPress
ILLUMINATING IDEAS
EMPOWERING VOICES

ARPress
45 Dan Road Suite 5
Canton MA 02021

Hotline: 1(888) 821-0229
Fax: 1(508) 545-7580

Ordering Information:
Quantity sales. Special discounts are available on quantity purchases by corporations, associations, and others. For details, contact the publisher at the address above.

Printed in the United States of America.
ISBN-13:   Paperback   979-8-89389-933-7
             eBook   979-8-89389-932-0

Library of Congress Control Number: 2024921311

Dedication

This book is dedicated to the memory of the two most incredible women I have ever known my mother and grandmother.

My mom and best earthly friend, Dr. Ella P. Hood transitioned to her heavenly promotion and in all honesty, my life has drastically changed. My mom was the wind beneath my wings and biggest cheerleader. She taught me the importance of loving the Heavenly Father with all my heart and how to live a life of faith. I know that I will see you again.
I love you momma.

My Grandmother, Deaconess Connie G. Patterson saw ministry in me at the tender age of 12. She laid hands, prayed, prophesied, and demonstrated a life of godliness. I love you grandma and will see you again as well.

Lastly, to all the women who are madly in love with Jesus Christ and desire a stronger and intimate relationship with Him. As you read, allow me to minister to you to become God's Certain Woman.

Exaltation

I have been in Sharon's life since she was a teenager. One day she asked me if I would be her godmother, it made me so happy when she asked me that question as I began to look into her beautiful brown eyes. I was speechless just knowing she wanted me to be a part of her life.

Sharon has grown up to be such a God fearing, caring, and dedicated woman who walks in obedience to the voice of God.

She has a love for hurting people, and great compassion for those in the community that are destitute. Matthew 25:35-36 Jesus said, "I was hungry you and you gave me food; I was thirsty, and you gave me something to drink, I was a stranger and you brought me together with yourselves and welcomed and entertained and lodged me. I was naked and you clothed me I was sick, and you visited me with help and ministering care, I was in prison, and you came to see me."

Sharon is a great example to women who are business minded, and a great impact upon those who are faithfully preaching the Gospel and winning the lost souls.

I pray when you read this book you will be healed and truly blessed. I Love you, Sharon.

-Your Godmother,

Prophetess Emma Moore

CONTENTS

Acknowledgements

Prophetess Emma Moore, my godmother. You have been an intricate part of my life from an early age. God has used you to speak into my life and to cover me in prayer. You have been there during times of mountains and valleys. I love you mom.

Prophet Earl Buggs, my godfather. You have been such a blessing to me through the years. We have spent many days and countless hours talking about the goodness of our God. You have stretched me spiritually and for that I say thank you. I love you dad.

My husband, Dr. Swindell Edwards, my sons, Rosie and Bran, my youngest sister and friend, Taqwen Agurs, my New Life Community Church and Broadcasting family, my beautiful and wise senior friends, Apostle Shelia Livingston, Mother Rosa Poston, Mother Mattie Clark, Deacon James Smith and so many others. A hearty thanks to all for your continued support and prayers.

Foreword

"Love never gives up, never loses faith, is always hopeful, and endures through every circumstance" Corinthians 13:7

In this book, you will feel the love that has been planted, the hours of endurance, and grace that was given by God for this extraordinary journey that Pastor Sharon Covington Edwards has been on. She has given a little piece of herself and wanted to share it with the world.

As her sister I get to see this on a daily, which I am blessed to be part of. God has done phenomenal things through her for others as his vessel. As a little girl, I have always admired the realness she has showed when speaking to family, friends, or people in passing. She is not shy to spread the good news of God and his glory.

I am delighted for everyone to read, just a snippet of why I love this woman of God so much and how blessed I am to call her my sister.
I love you.

-Ms. Taqwen Agurs

Introduction

In *Luke 13* we read about a woman, not just any woman, but a certain woman. This woman had a curvature of the spine. She was bent over and unable to rise for eighteen years. I admire this woman because despite her deformity, she was a worshiper. Her individual worship was not enough. She desired a corporate worship.

Her habit was to attend worship and to seek the favor and help of God. I feel safe in saying she stood on the Word of God. Perhaps a few of her favorite scriptures were *Hebrew 10:25*, "And let us not neglect our meeting together, as some people do, but encourage and warn each other, especially now that the day of His coming back again is drawing near." *Amos 5:4,* "Seek me and ye shall live;" *Psalm 105:4,* "Seek the Lord and His strength seek His face evermore;" *Matthew 6:33,* "But seek ye first the Kingdom of God and His righteousness and all these things shall be added unto you."

Her faithfulness in worship attracted Jesus to her. He knew about her condition with all its pain, inconvenience and the great sacrifice she made to worship.

He reached out and touched her, and she was made straight. She stood upright. She was in the right place at the right time to receive from the Lord. She needed to be touched, healed and delivered, and she was.

Whatever the infirmity you face, be it depression, oppression, disturbance, confusion, low self-esteem, fear, unforgiveness, pride, envy, strife, jealousy, sickness, abuse, neglect, past hurts and past failures; I pray this book will bless, awaken and lift your spirits.

You are A Certain Woman!

HER TEMPLE

For all the people of my town know
That you are a virtuous woman

- Ruth 3:11c

Her Mind

A certain woman has the mind of Christ.
Her thoughts are fixed on what is true, honorable and right.
She has thoughts of things that are pure, lovely and admirable.
She thinks about things that are excellent and worthy of praise.

Her motto is:
Guard your thoughts because they become your words.
Guard your words because they become your actions.
Guard your actions because they become your character,
and guard your character because it determines your destiny.

I am that Certain Woman

Romans 12:2 (NKJV)

And do not be conformed to this world, but be transformed by the renewing of your mind, that you may prove what is that good and acceptable and perfect will of God.

I Corinthians 2:15-16 (NKJV)

(15) But he who is spiritual judges all things, yet he himself is rightly judged by no one.

(16) For who has known the mind of the Lord that he may instruct him? But we have the mind of Christ.

Isaiah 26:3 (NKJV)

You will keep him in perfect peace, whose mind is stayed on You, because he trusts in You.

Philippians 2:5 (NKJV)

Let this mind be in you which was also in Christ Jesus.

Her Eyes

A certain woman's eyes, the organs of sight.
are beautifully sculptured by the powerful
and detail-oriented hands of God.

Ah yes, the pupils, or the apples of the eyes, can express
a wide range of emotions, gladness with a twinkle to
sorrow with rivers of water flowing downward.

They can express the emotion of greed, lust,
or a soft look of understanding.

God knows the power of the eyes;
after all, they are the window to the soul.

Certain woman of God, guard your eyes;
set no wicked things before them.

Remember this:

Your eyes observe first, then your mind processes what the eyes have beheld.
You ponder it in your heart,
and if you are operating in the wrong emotion,
your feet run swiftly to perform it.
What is "it" in this sense?

SIN

"And if your eye causes you to sin, pluck it out
*and cast it from you." **(Matthew 18:9)***

This does not mean to remove your eyes, but to
remove the stumbling blocks that cause you to sin.
Use your eyesight wisely, see yourself and life as God sees it.

I am that Certain Woman

Revelation 3:18c (NKJV)

...And anointed your eyes with eye salve, that you may see.

Psalm 101:4 (NKJV)

A perverse heart shall depart from me; I will not know wickedness.

Psalm 119:18 (NKJV)

Open my eyes, that I may see wondrous things from Your Law.

Her Ears

A certain woman has circumcised ears.
She listens attentively to the voice of the Holy Spirit as he gently
speaks, giving her directions and instructions for her life.

She recalls when her ears were uncircumcised, and she could
only hear the voices of the world and the lies of the enemy.
The uncircumcised ears usually hate to hear the truth
when it is spoken because the truth often hurts.
Especially when you know deep inside your heart
what has been spoken is true.

Uncircumcised ears are the equivalent of "itching ears."
Oh yes, they are itching because they only want
to hear what they want to hear, and
when they want to hear it.

She recalls when she would say to herself, "Oh Lord,
here they come again talking about you need to change!"
But NOW since she has fallen in love with Jesus and
is in an intimate relationship with Him, she asked Him
to give her circumcised ears to hear His sweet voice.
He has done just that. That is why she is now
a certain woman with circumcised ears.

Ears that can hear the voice of her God.
Ears that are now willing to hear the truth, the
*kind of truth that makes you free. (**John 8:32**).*
Ears that are no longer "itching" to hear what is going
to make her always feel good. Now she is willing
to hear constructive criticism.

She says, "I want to hear whatever is going to help me
grow in my relationship with Jesus." She will be able to
have ears to hear the wise council of her mentors, men
and women of God at whose feet she can sit and
glean wisdom and knowledge.

I am that Certain Woman

Revelation 2:7 (NKJV)

He who has an ear, let him hear what the Spirit says to the churches. To him who overcomes I will give to eat from the tree of life, which is in the midst of the Paradise of God.

Luke 10:38-39 (NKJV)

(38) Now it happened as they went that He entered a certain village; and a certain woman named Martha welcomed Him into her house.

(39) And she had a sister called Mary, who also sat at Jesus' feet and heard His word.

Her Mouth/Tongue

*A certain woman guards the words that proceed
from her mouth. She knows that once words are
spoken, they cannot be retrieved.*

*This member she refers to as the cannon which
contains a torpedo. This pink, flapping flesh dangles
approximately two inches from her nose.*

Yapping and nagging

Talking without thinking

Fault finding and criticizing

talking without thinking

exaggerating and boasting

talking without thinking

lying, gossiping and slandering

talking without thinking

harsh speech and unkind words

talking without thinking

*The tongue is a little member that requires a lot
of attention and discipline. For the tongue to be
tamed, you must have a willingness to change. You must
be willing to yield this member to the Holy Spirit.
The enemy will say this is a difficult task, and it is for YOU. But it
is just right for God. He does his best work with difficult tasks.
My sister, if you are quick with the tongue and you desire to*

change in this area; pray this prayer now as well as daily.

*Father, I come to you in humble submission. You are the source
and the strength of my life and it is in You I live, move and
have my being. I confess today that my tongue needs to be tamed.
I speak quickly Lord and I speak words that are not edifying,
but words that destroy and are hurtful.*

*Father, I have sinned with my tongue.
I ask for your forgiveness today. It is my desire to speak words
of encouragement and wisdom, therefore Father, I yield my tongue
to you now. Guard my tongue I pray, in Jesus' name. Amen.*

*My sister, if you prayed this prayer, then give God praise
for what He has done. Thank Him for the change. Remember you must do
your part to be more conscientious of what you speak.*

*If you have spoken words to or about an individual that were hurtful
or harmful, then make the decision that you will ask
him or her for forgiveness. This can sometimes be difficult to do,
but swallow your pride and do it.*

You are that Certain Woman

Isaiah 6:5-7 (NLT)

(5) Then I said, "My destruction is sealed, for I am a sinful
man and a member of a sinful race. Yet, I have seen the King,
the Lord Almighty!"

(6) Then one of the seraphim flew over to the altar, and he picked
up a burning coal with a pair of tongs.

(7) He touched my lips with it and said, "See, this coal has touched
your lips. Now your guilt is removed, and your sins are forgiven."

Proverbs 18:7 (NKJV)

A fool's mouth is his destruction, and his lips are the snare of his soul.

Proverbs 21:23 (NKJV)

Whoever guards his mouth and tongue keeps his soul from troubles.

James 3:2-12 (NLT)

(2) We all make many mistakes, but those who control their tongues can also control themselves in every other way.
(3) We can make a large horse turn around and go wherever we want by means of a small bit in its mouth.
(4) And a tiny rudder makes a huge ship turn wherever the pilot wants it to go, even though the winds are strong.
(5) So also, the tongue is a small thing, but what enormous damage it can do. A tiny spark can set a great forest on fire.
(6) And the tongue is a flame of fire. It is full of wickedness that can ruin your whole life. It can turn the entire course of your life into a blazing flame of destruction, for it is set on fire by hell itself.
(7) People can tame all kinds of animals and birds and reptiles and fish.
(8) But no one can tame the tongue, it is an uncontrollable evil, full of deadly poison.
(9) Sometimes it praises our Lord and Father, and sometimes it breaks out into curses against those who have been made in the image of God.
(10) And so blessing and cursing come pouring out of the same mouth. Surely, my brothers and sisters, this is not right!
(11) Does a spring of water bubble out with both fresh water and bitter water?
(12) Can you pick olives from a fig tree or figs from a grapevine? No, and you can't draw fresh water from a salty pool.

Her Heart

When I think of the heart, I think of a banana. A banana, you ask.

*Yes, a banana. Think of the outer peeling of a freshly picked
banana that is beautifully shaped, showing no sign of being
damaged, no bumps or bruises. It looks delectable,
but as you begin to slowly peel it, you see the
"real" banana which is brown and bruised.
The heart works in the same manner.*

*Let us look at a woman's outward appearance.
The hair is in place and topped with a stylish hat, and the suit is
pressed and creased. Shoes and handbag are a perfect match.
She looks good, just like a sanctified, tongue-talking,
devil chasing, church-going sister should,
but her heart is full of dirt and deceit.*

*Hearts which are hardened often refuse to change and
be regenerated by the power and the blood of Jesus Christ.
Your heart shows the real you, my sister:*

*How could such a small organ about the size
of your fist have such an impact on your life?*

*The Bible says the heart is the center of our being, for
out of it are the issues of life* **(Proverbs 4:23).**

*The heart is the wellspring of desires and decisions.
It determines our outward behavior, deeds and speech.
The heart is the center of emotions, human will and intellect.*

*A certain woman knows that without inward change and
conversion of the heart, she cannot do the will of the Lord.
When she watches over her heart with diligence and asks the
Lord to conform her heart to that of His, then the results of this
will be her ways being established in His favor and grace.*

I am that Certain Woman

Psalm 51:10 (NKJV)

Create in me a clean heart, O God, and renew a steadfast spirit within me.

Matthew 12:34b (NKJV)

For out of the abundance of the heart the mouth speaks.

Luke 6:45 (NLT)

A good person produces good deeds from a good heart, and an evil person produces evil deeds from an evil heart. Whatever is in your heart determines what you say.

Mark 7:20-23 (NLT)

(20) And then he added, "It is the thought-life that defiles you.

(21) For from within, out of a person's heart, come evil thoughts, sexual immorality, theft, murder,

(22) adultery, greed, wickedness, deceit, eagerness for lustful pleasure, envy, slander, pride, and foolishness.

(23) All these vile things come from within; they are what defile you and make you unacceptable to God."

Her Body

*A certain woman's body is the temple of the Holy Spirit.
It was designed to be set aside for Gods usage. Therefore,
she is determined to avoid any activity that will cause
her to be alienated from God.*

*She will not allow her body to be polluted with worldliness.
She is in the world, however, does not have to be a part of it.
She knows whatever is allowed to rule her body will
exemplify itself outwardly.
She is a holy woman of God by profession who
strives to be pure in spirit, body and soul.*

I am that Certain Woman

I Corinthian 3:16-17 (NKJV)

(16) Do you not know that you are the temple of God and that the Spirit of God dwells in you?

(17) If anyone defiles the temple of God, God will destroy him. For the temple of God is holy, which temple you are.

I Corinthian 6:18-20 (NKJV)

(18) Flee sexual immorality. Every sin that a man does is outside the body, but he who commits sexual immorality sins against his own body.

(19) Or do you not know that your body is the temple of the Holy spirit who is in you, whom you have from God, and you are not your own?

(20) For you were bought at a price; therefore glorify God in your body and in your spirit, which are God's.

I Corinthian 9:27 (NKJV)

But I discipline my body and bring it into subjection, lest, when I have preached to others, I myself should become disqualified.

Her Attire

A certain woman knows what looks good on her.
She understands her clothing does not make her,
she makes the clothing.

She knows how to be stylish, yet she is not compromising
or seductive in her attire.

No, it is not necessary to wear the long dress to the shoe tops,
the doily atop her head, no makeup, or jewelry.
That' not holy, that's ugly.

A certain woman knows that Jesus Christ looks at
the heart of an individual not the attire.

Yes, my sister, the attire is important, but it is not the key to
salvation or the key to having a right relationship with God.

Focus on being clothed with God's strength, humility,
Love, dignity and integrity.

I am that Certain Woman

I Timothy 2:9-10 (NLT)

(9) And I want women to be modest in their appearance.
They should wear decent and appropriate clothing and not draw
attention to themselves by the way they fix their hair or by wearing
gold or pearls or expensive clothes.

(10) For women who claim to be devoted to God should make
themselves attractive by the good things they do.

Isaiah 61:10 (KJV)

I will greatly rejoice in the Lord, my soul shall be joyful in my
God; for He hath clothed me with the garments of salvation, He
hath covered me with the robe of righteousness, as a bridegroom
decketh himself with ornaments, and as a bride adorneth herself
with her jewels.

MATTERS OF
THE HEART

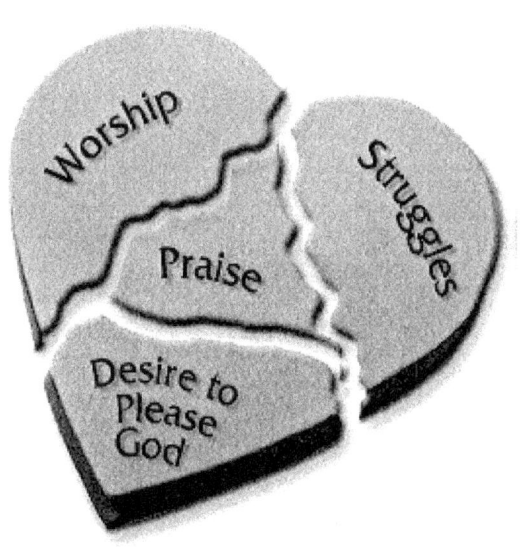

Create in me a clean heart, O God.
Renew a right spirit within me.
Psalm 51:10

Her Struggles

A certain woman praises her God during
her present struggles. She recalls this is what
she did to conquer the struggles of the past.
Praise, praise, a sacrifice of praise!

She continues to say to herself: "A different struggle,
same God, a different struggle same God."
He never changes. He has proven himself to
her so many times before. She has history with HIM.

She has been reading and studying the Word of God
and now she must work the Word.

Praise, praise, a sacrifice of praise!
Decree the Word of God!
Stand on the Word!
Declare the Word of God!
Stand on the Word!
Praise, praise, a sacrifice of praise!

She knows this is not the reaction the enemy expects
of her. "No, devil," she says, "I will not crack, crumble
or die; nor will I doubt my God."

He delivered once and He will do it again. Right on time!
My sister, sketch these words upon your heart. The struggles
you are presently facing are tools to make you stronger.
Your Heavenly Father knows when enough is enough.

Go through under the power and the authority of God.
You are a winner in Jesus!
These struggles are struggles of opportunities
for future victories.

I am that Certain Woman

1 Peter 1:7 (NLT)

These trials are only to test your faith, to show that it is strong and pure. It is being tested as fire tests and purifies gold - and your faith is far more precious to God than mere gold. So if your faith remains strong after being tried by fiery trials, it will bring you much praise and glory and honor on the day when Jesus Christ is revealed to the whole world.

Romans 8:28 (NLT)

And we know that God causes everything to work together for the good of those who love God and are called according to His purpose for them.

Psalms 94:17-19 (NKJV)

(17) Unless the Lord had been my help, My soul would soon have settled in silence.

(18) If I say, "My foot slips," Your mercy, O Lord will hold me up.

(19) In the multitude of my anxieties within me, Your comforts delight by soul.

Her Worship

Worship equals worthship. Worthship says,
Lord, you are worthy to be reverenced and honored.
There is none like You among the heavens or the earth.
A certain woman is aware of this attribute of God.

The worship of a certain woman is God-centered,
not man centered. It is not lip service, but it is
worship from the heart. Remember there are no good
things in the flesh. Therefore, do not worship the Lord in it.

As you worship, do not stay in the outer court,
but worship until you move into the holy of holies.
Absolutely no flesh can enter the holy of holies, therefore
your voice is no longer needed when you move into
this dimension of worship.

Bask in His presence and allow the peace and the spirit
of the Lord to encompass and embrace you.
What pleasure, joy and peace are found there.

Again, true worship is the road that leads to the holy of holies.
True worship takes place in the spirit. It will cause you to
draw near to God in gratitude for what He has done.

When true worship takes place, it becomes a sweet aroma
to the Lord. His presence will hover over you as
you worship from your heart and spirit.

The more you worship, the more the Lord has in store for you.
My sister, I urge you to become a true worshiper.

Yes, praise is what you do, however, worship is who you are.
Certain woman of God, please do not allow anyone or anything
to hinder worship from becoming a way of life for you.

I am that Certain Woman

Psalm 29:2 (NKJV)

Give unto the Lord the glory due unto His name; worship
the Lord in the beauty of holiness.

Psalm 95:6-7 (NKJV)

(6) Oh come, let us worship and bow down; let us kneel before
the Lord our Maker.

(7) For He is our God, and we are the people of His pasture, and
the sheep of His hand.

Her Praise

*A certain woman praises her God continually. These praise
breaks are like drinking a caffeinated soft drink;
they take you to a higher plain of gratitude.*

*My sister, there will be days when you feel praising God is in vain,
especially when it "appears" as if the situation is not changing.
When faced with difficult days the enemy will whisper subtle statements
such as, "You are too depressed, too unhappy or too stressed to
praise God." He will say, "What's the use, it is not getting better,
as a matter of fact, it is getting worse."*

*My advice beloved is to ignore the lies of the enemy.
He is a liar, cheater, deceiver and a thief.
He wants to steal your peace and your praise, do not
allow him to do so.*

*The magnitude of your praise should never be determined
by your feelings. Push your feelings aside and offer unto God
a sacrifice of praise. A sacrifice of praise speaks volumes.*

*It announces to the enemy, you will not focus on the problem;
but you will look to the problem solver, Jesus Christ!
When you praise, it expresses to God your appreciation and
understanding of His worth. It is your way of saying
thank you Lord, for your divine nature and awesomeness.
Your inward gratefulness becomes exemplified through
your outward expression of praise.*

*So, what are your waiting for? Praise, praise, praise!
Give unto the Lord a sacrifice of praise!*

I am that Certain Woman

Psalm 9:1-2 (NLT)

(1) I will thank you, Lord, with all my heart; I will tell of all the marvelous things You have done.

(2) I will be filled with joy because of You. I will sing praises to Your name, O Most high.

Psalm 103:1-3 (NLT)

(1) Praise the Lord, I tell myself; with my whole heart, I will praise His holy name.

(2) Praise the Lord, I tell myself; and never forget the good things He does for me.

(3) He forgives all my sins and heals all my diseases.

Psalm 104:1 (NLT)

Praise the Lord, I tell myself; O Lord my God, how great You are! You are robed with honor and with majesty.

Her Desire to Please God

A certain woman is a God pleaser, not a man pleaser.
She knows her God is a jealous God, therefore her desire
is to be totally committed to Him.

My sister, you must be willing to handle God's business first.
He will handle yours in His perfect timing.

***Matthew 6:33 (NLT)** states, "And He will give you all*
you need from day to day if you live for Him and make
the Kingdom of God your primary concern."

***Romans 8:5-8 (NLT)** states, "Those who are dominated by the sinful*
nature think about sinful things, but those who are controlled by the
Holy Spirit think about things that please the Spirit."

If your sinful nature controls your mind, there is death.
But if the Holy Spirit controls your mind, there is life and peace.
For the sinful nature is always hostile to God. It never did obey
God's laws, and it never will. That is why those who are still under
the control of their sinful nature can never please God.

You are not your own. Thank God for the shed blood of
Jesus Christ that washes our sins away.

He made the sacrifice for you. The ransom has been paid for you.
He loves you so much. Knowing this, why would you not want to
serve, worship and please such an awesome God?

I ask are you willing to put your agenda aside
And concentrate on the agenda of God?
There is a mandate and a calling on your life my sister.
Will you heed the call and work in the Kingdom to bring
Pleasure and glory unto the King?

God must be your priority if you expect to receive the
Fullness of His peace and blessing in your life.

I am that Certain Woman

I Thessalonians 2:4b (NLT)

Our purpose is to please God, not people. He is the one who examines the motives of our hearts.

I John 3:22 (NLT)

And we will receive whatever we request because we obey Him and do the things that please him.

ONLY GOD
CAN SATISFY

The fruit of the spirit is love, joy, peace,
Longsuffering, kindness, goodness, faithfulness,
Gentleness, and self control.
-Galatians 5:22

Her Thirst

A certain woman is thirsty for the living water that only her God can supply. She desires to drink from His fountain which never runs dry. She knows this water will refresh and revive her.

This water offers her something beyond her own human ability.

I am that Certain Woman

Psalm 42:1-2a (NLT)

As the deer pants for streams of water, so I long for you, O God.

(2a) I thirst for God, the living God.

Revelations 21:6 (NKJV)

And He said unto me, "It is done. I am Alpha and Omega, the beginning and the end. I will give unto him that is athirst of the fountain of the water of life freely."

Her Hunger

A certain woman has a desire to get closer to her God.

For me personally, there was a time in my life when this was not so.
I hungered for earthly things, and God was somewhere in between.

My sister, let me be the first to tell you, struggles, trials
and tribulations have a way of driving you to seek the love,
comfort and shelter of Jesus Christ, the rock that is higher than you.

The more I prayed, praised and studied my Bible, the more I matured
in my relationship with God. I realized my spiritual cup was only
half full. I concluded in order to receive the peace and joy I desired
I had to seek God with all my heart, spirit and mind.
I had to want Him more than anything else in the world.
I discovered His wonderful attributes and tender loving care.
NOW, I crave God. I am hungry for Him.
The more of himself He reveals to me the more I desire.
MORE of Him, less of me.
More, Lord, More!

I am that Certain Woman

Matthew 5:6 (NKJV)

Blessed are those who hunger and thirst for righteousness,
for they shall be filled.

HER
CONNECTIONS

How wonderful it is, how pleasant, when
Brothers (sisters) live together in harmony!
-Psalm 133:1

Her Sisters

A certain woman has a genuine love for sisters in the spirit. Pecan, olive, chocolate, or peachy skin tones, it matters not to her of their ethnicity, shape or size as long as she has a known intimate relationship with the lover of her soul, Jesus Christ.

She celebrates her sisters instead of tolerating them. She speaks truth not falsehood. She edifies her sisters and refuses to destroy them with harmful words or deeds. She intercedes for her sisters. Jealousy? What's that? Of course not!

She is overjoyed when her sisters succeed and never feels threatened by it. She's never afraid to compliment her sisters. She applauds them and is determined to be the human support her sisters need when facing struggles.

She stands on the sidelines with pom-poms in hand chanting: "You go sisters, go!"

I reiterate, there is no need to feel intimated when another sister is working and is successful in a particular area of the kingdom.

My sister, there remain vacancies in the kingdom of God that need to be filled. Apply for one today and get to work.

Do what the Lord has assigned to your hands. Get it done with a spirit of excellence and for His glory only.

I say, "Go, My Sister, Go!"

I am that Certain Woman

Proverbs 17:17 (NKJV)

A friend loves at all times, and a brother is born for adversity.

Proverbs 27:17 (KJV)

Iron sharpeneth iron; so a man sharpeneth the countenance of his friend.

Her Ministry (her calling)

*There are many in the body of Christ, each with various
giftings and callings. God has purposed you to play a vital
part in the enhancement of His kingdom.*

*As a certain woman of God, you should be willing to do
whatever the Lord has called and assigned you to do.
I pray you do so without hesitation.*

*Sometimes to stall for time, because we are fearful of
doing assignments that call us out of our comfort zones
we tend to say "I'm praying about it."
There is no need to pray about what you already know.
Stop procrastinating, get up and get to work! God has need of you.*

*Listen, my sister, God has already provided you
with the anointing to do the assignment.*

*You are AAA (anointed, appointed and approved).
Whatever God has called you to do, do it with
all of your might, spirit, body and soul.
Be who you are and no one else.*

*Do what you do, not to be seen, for position, nor power; but for
the glory of God, remember your gifts will make room for you.
It is difficult to walk in stilettos, when all you have ever worn
are sneakers and sandals. In other words, it's never necessary to walk nor
work in another's anointing.*

*As you work in your ministry, never compete with other sisters
in the kingdom. Instead of competing with her, find ways
you can assist, complete, boost, pray and motivate
her to do her best in her ministry assignments.*

What you make happen for others, God will make happen for you.
There's plenty of work to be done in the kingdom. The question is
"Are you doing your part?"

I am that Certain Woman

Ecclesiastes 9:10 (KJV)

Whatsoever thy hand findeth to do, do it with thy might; for there is no work, nor device, nor knowledge, nor wisdom, in the grave, whither thou goest.

John 9:4 (KJV)

I must work the works of Him that send Me, while it is day: the night cometh, when no man can work.

Proverbs 18:9 (KJV)

He also that is slothful in his work is brother to him that is a great waster.

Colossians 3:17, 23 (KJV)

(17) And whatsoever ye do in word or deed, do all in the name of the Lord Jesus, giving thanks to God and the Father by Him. (23) And whatsoever ye do, do it heartily, as to the Lord, and not unto men.

Matthew 5:16 (KJV)

Let your light so shine before men, that they may see your good works, and glorify your Father which is in heaven.

Hebrew 6:10 (KJV)

For God is not unrighteous to forget your work and labor of love, which you have showed toward His name, in that ye have ministered to the saints, and do minister.

THE
BRANCHES
OF HER LIFE

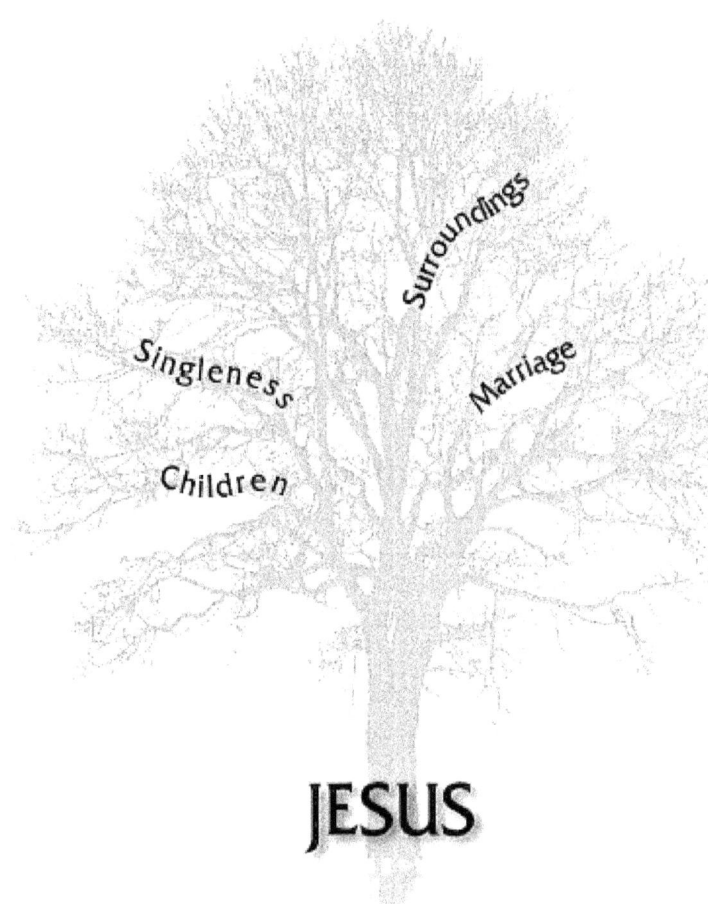

Surroundings

Singleness

Marriage

Children

JESUS

For no one can lay any other foundation
than the one we already have – Jesus Christ
-I Corinthians 3:11

Her Surroundings

A certain woman is cautious of her surroundings.
She knows she is fearfully, beautifully,
and wonderfully designed by her creator.
She is determined to let that beauty shine all around her.

My sister, refuse to allow negativity to contaminate your
surroundings. When negativity is allowed to invade your
space, it causes you to become a prisoner of circumstances.

We have all been there and have experienced
firsthand the residue negativity leaves behind.
It is so vitally important for you to be cautious about those
you associate with. The old cliché of association brings
about assimilation is very much a reality.

Surround yourself with individuals who are capable of
enhancing you, individuals who are on a higher level than you.
In doing so, what happens is that he or she is able
to pour into your spirit.

*Remember Mary and Martha in **Luke 10.** Jesus came to*
pay them a visit. Martha was scurrying around to
make everything "just right" for Jesus.
But her sister, Mary, saw the bigger picture.

The revelation for her was this man has something I need.
He has the capability of pouring into my spirit.
I'm half full, but He has what I need to reach my destiny.
I must sit at His feet and eat spiritually. I must glean from him.
He holds the key to the door I need opened.

There will always be those who will fail to understand you and why
you do what you do. They will not understand your hunger and thirst
for more. They are satisfied with the very minimum spiritually,
but you want and desire more.

Luke 10:40 exemplifies this. But Martha was cumbered about much serving, and came to him, and said, "Lord, dost thou not care that my sister hath left me to serve alone? Bid her therefore that she help me."

*Jesus summarized it so beautifully in verses **41-42** "And Jesus answered and said unto her, Martha, Martha, thou art careful and troubled about many things: but one thing is needful; and Mary hath chosen that good part, which shall not be taken away from her."*

What Martha was doing was good, but what Mary did was better. She was surrounding herself with greatness.

My sister; surround yourself with the two positives: Positive thinkers and positive speakers. And watch how your environment will blossom like a flower with the beauty of holiness and success for the glory of God.

I am that Certain Woman

Proverbs 23:7a (NKJV)

For as he thinks in his heart, so is he.

Proverbs 13:20 (NLT)

Whoever walks with the wise will become wise; whoever walks with fools will suffer harm.

Psalm 139:13-16 (NLT)

(13) You made all the delicate, inner parts of my body and knit me together in my mother's womb.

(14) Thank you for making me so wonderfully complex! Your workmanship is marvelous and how well I know it.

(15) You watched me as I was being formed in utter seclusion, as I was woven together in the dark of the womb.

(16) You saw me before I was born. Every day of my life was recorded in your book. Every moment was laid out before a single day had passed.

Her Single Lifestyle

I Corinthians 7:6-7 (NLT) This is my only suggestion. It's not meant to be an absolute rule. I wish everyone could get along without marrying, just as I do. But we are not all the same. God gives some the gift of marriage, and others he gives the gift of singleness.

Despite what others may say, being single is a gift from God. You may have a desire to be married, but right now, my sister, be content in your singleness.

As Naomi was busy working in the fields, you too must be busy working in the kingdom of God.

As a single woman, you should be committed to your relationship with God. At this time, he wants you to himself.

He is a jealous God, and he has much for you to do for Him. He is omniscient and has everything in His control. He knows what you desire, however, timing is everything.

When we get in a hurry and start looking at our age and the biological clocks, we think time is running out. But I must tell you that all time belongs to God. He knows the number of hairs on your head and he is well aware of your age and your "clock." Rest in Him and trust his better judgement.

If you want to experience headache and heartache, then get married prematurely. I guarantee you as time progresses you will say to yourself, "I wish I had waited."

Take time right now and reflect on the past. You recall the time you walked ahead of God, doing your thing and having it your way? Ms. Burger King, how did it leave you feeling? I will tell you: wishing you could turn back the hand of time.

Listen, beloved, the enemy wants to derail your spiritual train.
He wants you to wreck. He wants you to yield to temptation.
In a nutshell he is like a bloodhound, sniffing out your anointing
to devour it. He wants you to lose your anointing.
What better way to lose the anointing than going
before God and doing things your way?

Sisters, the anointing costs, it is not free. The greater the
anointing the greater the cost. Please do not jeopardize losing your
anointing to satisfy the flesh. God will not get out of line to bless you.
Maintain your position and stay focused.

If you feel yourself slipping, immediately pray and call a stronger,
trustworthy sister in Christ to pray and intercede for you.
We are our brother's keeper. **Romans 15:1** *state*
"We then that are strong ought to bear the infirmities.
of the weak and not to please ourselves."
Our Heavenly Father's umbrella of grace and mercy is a
good place to be during those times when you feel
as if your singleness is a "curse."
Ask the Him to transform your mind and
conform your will to His and to keep you.
Become the bride of God first, and in time Boaz not bozo will
find you.

I am that Certain Woman

I Corinthians 7:8-9 (NLT)

(8) Now I say to those who aren't married and to widows - it is
better to stay unmarried, just as I am.

(9) But if they can't control themselves, they should go ahead
and marry. It's better to marry than to burn with lust.

II Corinthians 6:14-16a (NLT)

(14) Don't team up with those who are unbelievers. How can goodness be a partner with wickedness? How can light live with darkness?

(15) What harmony can there be between Christ and the Devil? How can a believer be a partner with an unbeliever?

(16a) And what union can there be between God's temple and idols? For we are the temple of the living God.

Jeremiah 29:11 (NKJV)

For I know the thoughts that I think toward you, says the Lord, thoughts of peace and not of evil, to give you a future and a hope.

Philippians 4:11 (KJV)

Not that I speak in respect of want: for I have learned, in whatsoever state I am, therewith to be content.

Her Husband (marriage)

*The married certain woman is deeply in love with her husband.
He is a Godly, loving, kind and gentle man. He is her earthly
provider, her king, and her covering. How could she not be
submissive to such a man? He is the one who lays hands on
her and intercedes on her behalf, and she does likewise for him.*

*They come together in prayer, in fasting and in studying.
Gods written word. They seek him daily for guidance on
how to love and care for each other as well as the home.
The two are now one wrapped in the loving arms
of their Heavenly Father.*

*She asks God to bless her hands, to esteem her
home and her husband.*

*She is a bragger of the God in him, not a nagger.
She is a lifter of his spirit, not an oppressor.
She is a lover and a friend, not a fighter and an enemy.
She is a helper to him, the shoulder for him
to lean upon, not a hinder.
She is a communicator, not a dominator.*

*She is his favorite girl and biggest fan. He can count on her to
"be there." She understands him and he her. She will be the positive
in his life and not the negative. She is his queen and he is her king.*

I am that Certain Woman

Genesis 2:22-24 (NLT)

(22) Then the lord God made a woman from the rib and brought her to Adam.

(23) "At last!" Adam exclaimed. "She is a part of my own flesh and bone! She will be called 'woman, because she was taken out of a man."

(24) This explains why a man leaves his father and mother and is joined to his wife, and the two are united into one.

Proverbs 18:22 (NLT)

The man who finds a wife finds a treasure and receives favor from the Lord.

Proverbs 31:30-31 (NLT)

(30) Charm is deceptive, and beauty does not last; but a woman who fears the Lord will be greatly praised.

(31) Reward her for all she has done. Let her deeds publicly declare her praise.

Proverbs 14:1 (NLT)

A wise woman builds her house; a foolish woman tears hers down with her own hands.

Her Children

A certain woman knows that her children are gifts from God.
She seeks God for maternal instincts on how to be
a Godly mother before and after she has children.

In the words of Charles H. Spurgeon, she is training her
children in the way in which she should have gone herself.

A certain woman intercedes for her children in prayer and
decrees them to be covered under the blood of Jesus Christ.
She openly prays and praises God before her children.

She teaches them the importance of family prayer and devotion.
She always leads by example.

A certain woman lives a Godly life before her children. She knows
she cannot speak a different language in her lifestyle.
Actions speak louder than words.

She realizes her children are observing her actions and motives.
She always leads by example.

A certain woman loves her children and expresses her
love by encouraging, correcting, applauding,
communicating and celebrating them.

She then leads by example.

I am that Certain Woman

Deuteronomy 6:5-9 (NLT)

(5) And you must love the Lord your God with all your heart, all your soul, and all your strength.

(6) And you must commit yourselves wholeheartedly to these commands I am giving you today.

(7) Repeat them again and again to your children. Talk about them when you are at home and when you are away on a journey, when you are lying down and when you are getting up again.

(8) Tie them to your hands as a reminder, and wear them on your forehead.

(9) Write them on the doorposts of your house and on your gates.

Proverbs 22:6 (NKJV)

Train up a child in the way he should go, and when he is old he will not depart from it.

Psalm 127:3-5a (NKJV)

(3) Behold, children are a heritage from the Lord, the fruit of the womb is a reward.

(4) Like arrows in the hands of a warrior, so are the children of one's youth.

(5a) Happy is the man who has his quiver full of them.

HER
INSPIRATION

The flowers are springing up,
And the time of singing birds has come
- Song of Solomon 2:12

Her Attitude

Attitude has always equaled altitude. There is nothing worse than a Christian sister with a horrible attitude.

A sister can be as beautiful as the Queen of Sheba on the outside, but if her attitude resembles the city dump, who wants to be acquainted or surrounded with such smelly nonsense?

I know there are times when "folks" will provoke you, but you must learn to handle the situation with the right attitude.

Listen, somebody out of the bunch must exemplify the proper attitude, so it might as well be you.

You can make your point my sister without the ATTITUDE!

If you know this is an area in which you need a major tune up, then you should sincerely make up your mind that you will change and then move toward that change.

Don't forget to take it to the Lord in prayer. Be honest with the Heavenly Father. He already knows you need an attitude adjustment. He's waiting for you to confess it.

I am that Certain Woman

James 4:10 (NLT)

When you bow down before the Lord and admit your dependence on him, he will lift you up and give you honor.

John 3:30 (NLT)

He must become greater and greater, and I must become less and less.

Her Faith

What is a certain woman's faith?
Her faith is a reliance, loyalty and complete trust in God.

Her faith has a beginning and an ending. It begins by
believing in the character of God, who He is, and it ends by
believing God's promises that He will do what He says.

He is not slack concerning his promises.
She walks by faith and not by sight.
If you can see it, it's not faith!

A certain woman knows that true faith is demonstrated by
believing even though it has not materialized yet. She reminds
herself that faith goes beyond believing; it results in action.
A certain woman understands the importance of faith
building. She builds her faith by studying the word of God
and lying prostrate before Him daily in prayer.

Faith comes by hearing and hearing by the Word of God.
The Word of God is the umbilical cord to her reaching
her destiny in God through faith.

I am that Certain Woman

Hebrews 11:1 (NKJV)

Now faith is the substance of things hoped for, the evidence of things not seen.

Hebrews 11:6a (NKJV)

But without faith it is impossible to please him.

Matthew 17:19-20 (NLT)

(19) Afterward the disciples asked Jesus privately, "Why couldn't we cast out that demon?"

(20) "You didn't have enough faith," Jesus told them. "I assure you, even if you had faith as small as a mustard seed you could say to this mountain, 'Move from here to there, and it would move. Nothing would be impossible."

Romans 1:17 (KJV)

For therein is the righteousness of God revealed from faith to faith: as it is written, the just shall live by faith.

Her Determination

Give up? Don't you dare think about it, my sister!
You have come entirely too far to throw in the towel now.

Remember the promise of the Heavenly Father.
"I'll never leave you, nor forsake you."

How could you forget what you have promised Him?
"Lord, I'm staying with you no matter what."
So why are you thinking about giving up?

You are God's certain woman, his daughter
in Zion, and you are not a quitter.

You are pregnant with possibilities, I decree and
declare you will give birth now.

Adjust your breathing, don't panic, relax.
God is still with you.
He is your coach.
Come on push!
You're tired? I know but push anyway!

You say, "I've tried once and I failed."
I say re-evaluate and try again.

Again, come on push!
You can do it. have confidence in you.

I declare to you today, my sister, you will give birth to
your spiritual babies. Your mind is resolute, so move
forward in the strength of God.

You are a mover!
You are shaker!
You are a winner!
You are determined!

I am that Certain Woman

Ephesians 4:23 (NKJV)

And be renewed in the spirit of your mind.

Proverbs 16:3 (KJV)

Commit thy works unto the Lord, and thy thoughts shall be established.

Isaiah 26:3 (KJV)

Thou wilt keep him in perfect peace, whose mind is stayed on Thee: because he trusteth in Thee.

Philippians 4:13 (NKJV)

I can do all things through Christ who strengthens me.

Her Wisdom:
An Understanding Heart

Wisdom is the ability to discern what is best and the strength of character to act upon that knowledge.

How does she obtain wisdom? First, it is obtained by reverencing the Lord, and then, by asking God for it.

She knows that wisdom is an action word, and she must be willing to apply it to all areas of her life.

This includes her relationships, friendships, business dealings, decisions and her finances.

No area is off limits to His wisdom.

When she applies wisdom to her life, it demonstrates. her understanding of seeking God in all things first, not after the fact.

She believes that He will give her the courage needed to follow the plans He has so skillfully mapped out for her.

A certain woman understands that wisdom brings fruit such as peace, prosperity, and security.

I am that Certain Woman

James 1:5 (NLT)

If you need wisdom, if you want to know what God wants you to do - ask him, and he will gladly tell you. He will not resent your asking.

James 3:13 (NLT)

If you are wise and understand God's ways, live a life of steady goodness so that only good deeds will pour forth. And if you don't brag about the good you do, then you will be truly wise!

Colossians 4:5 (NLT)

Live wisely among those who are not Christians, and make the most of every opportunity.

Proverbs 2:10 (NLT)

For wisdom will enter your heart, and knowledge will fill you with joy.

Proverbs 3:13 (NLT)

Happy is the person who finds wisdom and gains understanding.

Proverbs 4:5,7 (NLT)

(5) Learn to be wise, and develop good judgement. Don't forget or turn away from my words.

(7) Getting wisdom is the most important thing you can do! And whatever else you do, get good judgment.

Proverbs 8:11-12 (NLT)

(11) For wisdom is far more valuable than rubies. Nothing you desire can be compared with it.

(12) I, Wisdom, live together with good judgment. I know where to discover knowledge and discernment.

Proverbs 16:16 (NLT)

How much better to get wisdom than gold, and understanding than silver!

Her Dreams

A certain woman is a dreamer, a visionary, and a faith walker.
She sees herself already there through the eyes of faith.
(There) denotes her special place. A place that was
revealed to her by God in her dreams.

She ponders these dreams in her heart as she seeks God's
powerful hand to cause these dreams to move from the
corner of her mind into reality.

She must keep the dreams alive within her spirit.
She will not abort her dreams and her visions for her life.
She also refuses to allow others to toss them into a pit, left for dead.
It matters not what others think of her dreams,
because they were revealed to her.

Dream killers exist; therefore, she guards her dreams with
prayer and covers them with the blood of Jesus.

She trusts the voice of God to guide her as to whom to share
her dreams with, or if she should share them at all.
Her mama once said, "Baby, share your dreams once
they have been manifested."

I am that Certain Woman

Genesis 37:5-11, 18-20 (KJV)

(5) And Joseph dreamed a dream, and he told it his brethren: and they hated him yet the more.

(6) And he said unto them, Hear, I pray you, this dream which I have dreamed:

(7) For, behold, we were binding sheaves in the field, and, lo, my sheaf arose, and also stood upright; and, behold, your sheaves stood round about, and made obeisance to my sheaf.

69

(8) And his brethren said to him, Shalt thou indeed reign over us? Or shalt thou indeed have dominion over us? And they hated him yet the more for his dreams, and for his words.

(9) And he dreamed yet another dream, and told it his brethren, and said, Behold, I have dreamed a dream more; and behold the sun and the moon and the eleven stars made obeisance to me.

(10) And he told it to his father, and to his brethren: and his father rebuked him, and said unto him, What is this dream that thou hast dreamed? Shall I and thy mother and thy brethren indeed come to bow down ourselves to thee to the earth?

(11) And his brethren envied him; but his father observed the saying.

(18) And when they saw him afar off, even before he came near unto them, they conspired against him to slay him.

(19) And they said one to another, Behold, this dreamer cometh.

(20) Come now therefore, and let us slay him, and cast him into this pit, and we will say, some evil beast hath devoured him: and we shall see what will become of his dreams.

Isaiah 54:17 (KJV)

No weapon that is formed against thee shall prosper; and every tongue that shall rise against thee in judgment thou shalt condemn. This is the heritage of the servants of the Lord, and their righteousness is of Me, saith the Lord.

Philippians 4:13 (NKJV)

I can do all things through Christ who strengthens me.

Her Position, Her Identity

The certain woman of God is seated in heavenly places with Christ Jesus. What does this mean? It means that she has power and authority given to her by Adonai. He has power, so does she. He has authority, so does she. She is crafted in His image and His likeness.

It is the Heavenly Father's good pleasure to give her these heavenly benefits of power and authority to be used while she is in the earth realm. However, she must realize she possesses these benefits to be an effective overcomer.

*A certain woman understands her position in Christ Jesus. She does battles from this position. The enemy does not stand a chance of defeating her. Why? Because she **knows** her position.*

*She has power to do extraordinary things because she has been authorized to do so by Jesus Christ. The label above her heart reads: **Invincible and unconquerable**.*

Even when she is weak, she is strong by association. She knows it is not by might nor by power, but by the Spirit of the Living God. She is plugged into the King of all kings and the Lord of all lords, Jesus Christ.

I am that Certain Woman

Ephesians 2:6 (KJV)

And hath raised us up together and made us sit together in heavenly places in Christ Jesus.

Luke 12:32 (KJV)

Fear, not little flock; for it is your Father's good pleasure to give you the kingdom.

II Corinthians 12:8-9 (KJV)

(8) For this thing I besought the Lord thrice, that it might depart from me.

(9) And he said unto me, My grace is sufficient for thee: for my strength is made perfect in weakness.

Her Focus

A Certain Woman understands the importance of remaining focused to her call, to her passion. When one loses her passion, it is easy to drift away from the mission.

There will be others who will attempt to cast doubt wrapped in fear concerning her mission. However, she will not allow anyone to stand in her way and most of all she does not stand in her own way.

It is easy to be fixated on what she does not possess, however stay focused on the Heavenly Father and not the negativity. So, removed wrong thinking and speech; maintain the mind of Christ.

When she is certain that she has heard the reassuring voice of her best friend, Holy Spirit saying, "Drive and Go Forward," she does.

Passion is powerful, do not waste it because your passion has the potential to empower others to move into his or her passion.

I am created to do great things, therefore just getting by is not my portion.

I am a Certain Woman

Colossians 3:2 KJV

Set your affection on things above, not on things on the earth.

Proverbs 4:25 KJV

Let thine eyes look right on and let thine eyelids look straight before thee.

Her Walk

A certain woman dares to walk in faith with her God. She is not led by the flesh or the lust thereof.
She walks in truth, for HE is truth. She walks in love, for HE is love. She walks in righteousness, for HE is righteous. She walks in power, for HE is power. She walks in authority, for HE has all authority.
Although she is walking in faith, this does not exempt her from experiencing hurt, slander or pain despite the challenges she may face her walk with God continues.
She is not a walker of faith in public only, but in private as well. It is her private faithful prayer life that prepares her for her public faith walk. She is walking in the Spirit of God.
In what direction are you walking? Are you walking in the light or in darkness? Are you walking on the narrow road with the Spirit or the broad road of the adversary? Are you walking in faith or in fear and by your sight? Are you walking in the Spirit or after the flesh?

I am that Certain faith walking Woman

II Corinthians 5:7 KJV

For we walk by faith, not by sight.

Romans 8:1 KJV

There is therefore now no condemnation to those who are in Christ Jesus, who do not walk according to the flesh, but according to the Spirit.

I John 1:7 KJV

But if we walk in the light, as he is in the light, we have fellowship one with another, and the blood of Jesus Christ his Son cleanseth us from all sin.

Proverbs 1:1-3 KJV

(1) Blessed is the man that walketh not in the counsel of the ungodly, nor standeth in the way of sinners, nor sitteth in the seat of the

scornful.

(2) But his delight is in the law of the Lord; and in his law doth he meditate day and night.

(3) And he shall be like a tree planted by the rivers of water, that bringeth forth his fruit in his season; his leaf also shall not wither; and whatsoever he doeth shall prosper.

She is a Modern-Day Deborah

Deborah was used by God during a time when Israel had once again sinned against the Lord. Because of their sins, he allowed King Jabin along with his commander in chief, Sisera, an enemy to arise, overtake, rule, and make life extremely unbearable for them for twenty years.
Disobedience certain woman will always have a price tag attached to it. Can you pay the price? Israel realized they could not and began to cry out to God for deliverance and help.
The sovereign God answered their cry and raised up a leader and a prophetess by the name of Deborah.
Deborah was instrumental in steering Israel back to God. There are modern-day Deborahs holding this book and God has purposed to use you to steer and lead people to him.

Perhaps you may feel that this word is not for you because of feelings of inadequacy. Have you been comparing yourself to others and saying, "I do not measure up" or does fear have you in a choke hold position?
Have you have been rehearsing your lines for the one woman show starring you, saying to yourself," I am not smart or worthy enough."
I beg to differ my sister.
It is YOU, that from the womb of your mother he put the anointing of Deborah within you. It is YOU, that God has tapped for such a time as this to do great exploits for his glory.
It is YOU, that he has had hidden on the countryside or the back side of the desert. The journey to this place has been long and difficult. You have been misunderstood and perhaps had to walk alone.
These were just a few of the ingredients that made it possible for you to become a modern-day Deborah.

He has been preparing you for such a time as this to lead your unsaved loved ones, coworkers, and even your enemies to the foot of the cross. Yes, God used Deborah to sit in a place of leadership and authority as a judge. She held court if you will under a palm tree between Ramah, which means height and Bethel which means house of God in the hill country of Ephraim which means fruitful in the land of affliction.

It is time modern-day Deborah to soar to higher heights. You have been hidden in the house of God doing the "comfortable assignments," however, its time now to move to center stage.

I am a Certain Woman, I am a modern-day Deborah

Read the story of Deborah in Judges Chapter 4

Psalms 18:33 KJV

He maketh my feet like hinds' feet, and setteth me upon my high places.

Her Personal Notes

_____

_____

_____

_____

_____

_____

_____

_____

_____

_____

_____

_____

_____

_____

_____

_____

_____

_____

_____

_____

_____

_____

_____

_____